Day*walkS
Wyre Forest

a network of 20 linked footpath routes
exploring the forest, the hills and the dingles
west of the River Severn

by John Roberts

****
WALKWAYS
J S Roberts
8 Hillside Close, Bartley Green
Birmingham B32 4LT
****

DaywalkS: Wyre Forest
(Second Edition)

ISBN 0 947708 25 1

First Published 1987   ISBN 0 947708 15 4

WA*LKWAYS

DaywalkS Footpath Networks

This series now includes networks of walks in
Arden
Cannock Chase
Chaddesley Woods
Clent & Lickey Hills
Elan Valley
Tywyn & Aberdyfi
Bridgnorth - Kinver - Stourport
with more planned.

All but the last two are currently in folded A2
sheet format, sold in a plastic cover. They will
gradually be replaced by expanded networks covering
the same areas in book form, like this one.

Long Distance Routes

Full step by step guides for walking in either
direction with sketch maps. You can start at a
number of midway points and these routes often
connect with each other and other Long Distance
Footpaths. (All are folded A2 sheets folded to
A5, but Heart of England Way is a book.)

Llangollen to Bala
Bala to Snowdon
Birmingham to Ludlow
Ludlow to Rhayader
Rhayader to Aberystwyth
Birmingham to Church Stretton
Heart of England Way

8 Hillside Close, Bartley Green, Birmingham B32 4LT
(Send sae for current list & prices.)

To enjoy the best of the countryside

Join The Ramblers.

Explore the many hundreds of thousands of miles of Britain's beautiful footpaths and receive our exclusive Yearbook full of information on walking and places to stay.

Plus regular colour magazines and newsletters — free of charge.

You will also be entitled to valuable discounts at outdoor equipment shops.

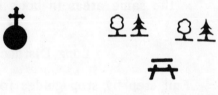

And at the same time you will be helping us to protect the countryside and to look after Britain's footpaths.

Contents

The Landscape

The Severn Valley forms the eastern boundary of this network of footpaths. The northern point is near Chorley Covert about five miles south of Bridgnorth. This is the last remnant of real woodland in that direction, although there are big, dense dingles fringing all the main streams. To the west Routes 4, 6 and 20 follow the edge of the forest which reaches almost to Cleobury Mortimer. In the south the walks are in the area of Rock which is clear of the forest, and the last bit of woodland is Burnt Wood.

Two main streams flow east across the forest into the Severn. In the north the Borle Brook in the Chorley - Highley area, and the Dowles Brook running more or less from Cleobury to Bewdley. Each has many tributaries which run (roughly) from north and south into them. The overall effect is to break up the landscape into a complex system of blocks of hills between deep valleys. However the ground also shows a general pattern beneath this, and here I am being very approximate, of two ridges running north - south, parallel with the Severn. The nearest to the river runs through high points of 130 to 170 metres between Chelmarsh and Callow Hill. The second, further west, has tops between 230 and 180 metres between Chorley and Rock.

What all this means is a very hilly landscape with some of the best and most varied walking in the Midlands.

The soil is mainly sandy gravel deposits dumped onto a sandstone base by the glaciers as they retreated north some 10,000 years ago. The predominent tree is durmast or sessile oak, as in much of the ancient Midland forest, allthough its cousin, the English Oak occupies the more moist and fertile sites. But the Forestry Commission have owned the Wyre since 1925 and the planting havesting and replanting has included Larch, Douglas Fir, Beech and Scots and Lodgepole Pine. Managing for themselves are Willows, Birch and Mountain Ash. Wildfife includes dormice, fallow deer, huge wood ants which build three foot high nests of wood fragments and a rich variety of birds and plants.

Each route in this network has a few comments attached and notes on points of interest, but this is a book of walks, not a comprehensive guide to the Wyre. There are many books and leaflets which will tell you more. Find out about the Norman Royal Forest, the draconian Forest Laws, the effects of the Industrial Revolution, local industries such as coppicing, tanning and charcoal burning, the long history of the port of Bewdley with its bow hauliers, trow builders and buildings, and the plants, animals, birds and insects that make up the Wyre.

In Bewdley there is a bookshop, a Museum and a Tourist Information Office. At Callow Hill the Forestry Commission have a Visitor Centre.

****

*Daywalks
Wyre Forest

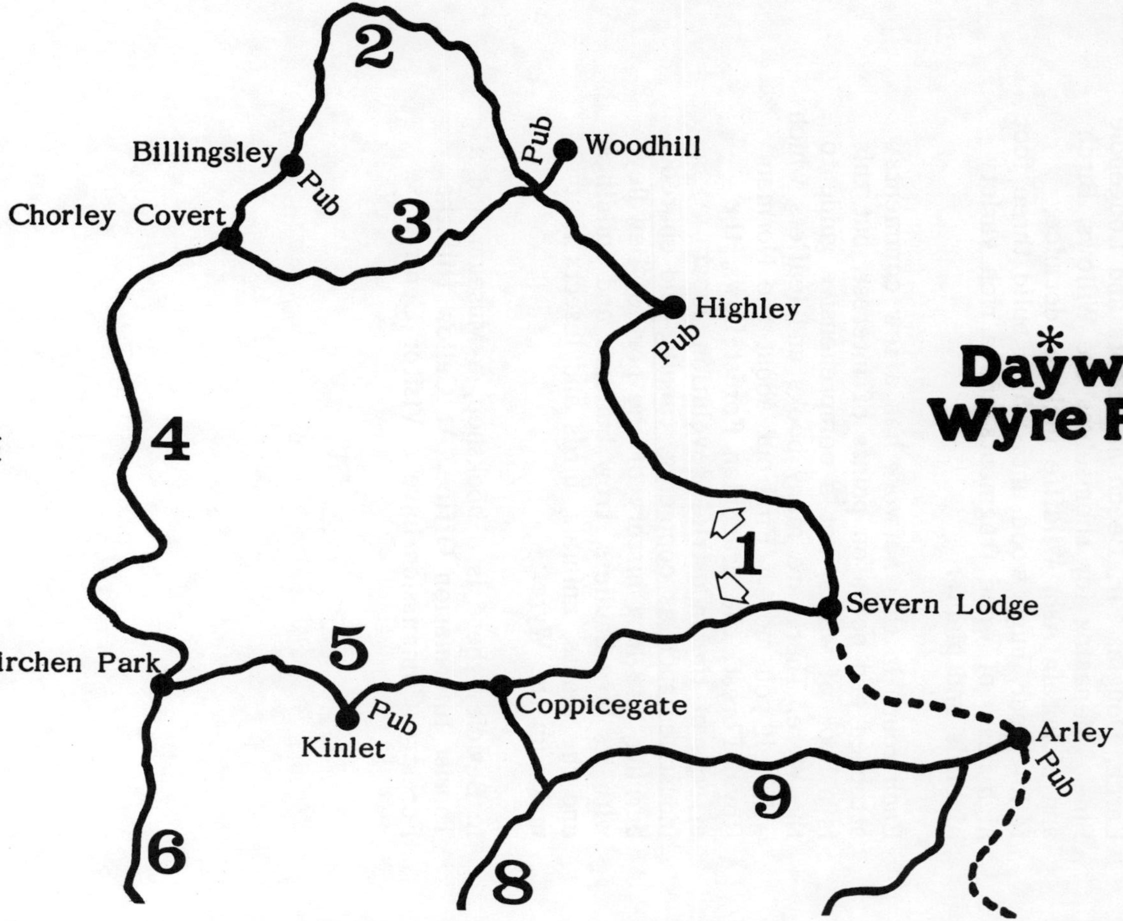

Arley **Pub**

Severn Lodge

Highley **Pub**

Woodhill **Pub**

Billingsley **Pub**

Chorley Covert

Coppicegate

Kinlet **Pub**

Birchen Park

2

3

1

5

4

6

8

9

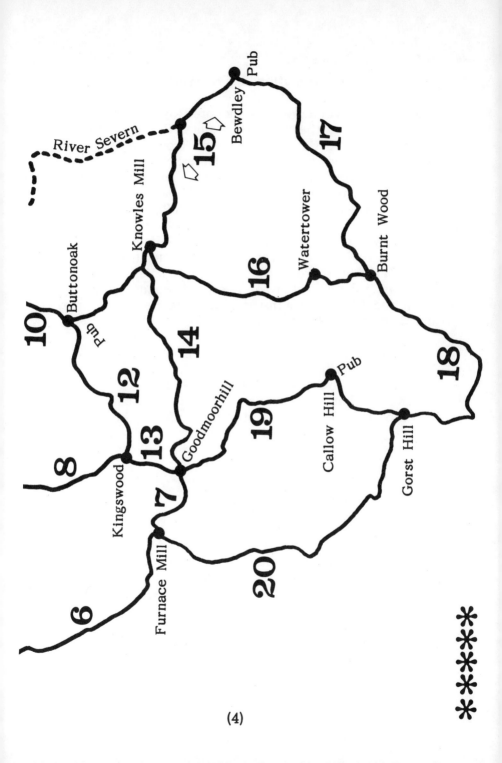

Information & Transport

Most people will travel to the area by car and drive to one of the Junction Points. But you can come by bus to Bewdley and walk from there, or go on to Water Tower or Callow Hill. Several operators serve the Forest area from Kidder -minster; contact the Tourist Information Offices at Bewdley ((0299 403573) or Kidderminster (0562 829400).

Rail travel is not only possible, but delightful. BR runs to Kidderminster of course (enquiries 021 643 2711) but there is also the Severn Valley Railway, running volunteer operated steam trains from the BR Kidderminster station to Bewdley, Arley and Highley (0299 403816).

You can walk both banks of the Severn between Bewdley and Highley; the west bank is more attractive. Obviously the routes need no description but you can use them at links between parts of this network. It may be useful to know where you can cross the river:

> Bewdley .. roadbridge
> Arley .. footbridge only
> Highley .. footbridge only
> Bridgnorth .. roadbridge

There is a good network of minor roads and I point out whether parking space is available at each Junction Point. In some cases you will be using grass verges or other odd spots. Park with great care;
> USE a car park wherever possible
> NEVER obstruct narrow lanes
> ASSUME that field gates WILL be used.

You will need

* A MAP

An Ordnance Survey Landranger (1.25ins/1mile) sheet 138 (Kidderminster & Wyre Forest), or for people who love maps the Pathfinder (2.5ins/1mile) sheets SO 67/77 (Wyre Forest & Cleobury Mortimer) and SO 68/78 (Highley). There is a sketch map of each route with the directions so you should manage very well with the Landranger.

* CLOTHING & GEAR

Yes of course. What I meant was, suitable clothing for walking. Your own experience will be the best guide in the long run but if you have none, consider these points.

(1) Boots. Most people seems to prefer them at most times of year; go for the lightest that you can find. Trainers are excellent in dry weather and make progress so much easier. In fact, if it rains and rains even your boots will fill, and I think wet trainers are lighter and more bearable than wet boots. Think about it.

(2) Socks. You don't necessarily need two pairs, but a good thickness of woolly padding is a great comfort. The traditional grey rough wool "rag sock" is hardwearing and reasonably thick, but that is about all. Try loop pile socks, the best invention since feet.

(3) Gaiters are good news in bad weather, and can keep you comfortable through mud, flood and undergrowth. You can keep them on in all but the hotest weather.

(4) Avoid jeans because they are cut too close for comfortable walking. Denim may be fine in California where it was first used by a Mr Levi to make working trousers, but here it is hot in summer, cold in winter, holds the damp and is in any case heavy and stiff. In summer try polycotton tousers which are light and dry in no time. In colder weather corduroy is not bad.

(5) Take a waterproof, preferably hooded and long enough to reach down to your gaiters.

(6) Take a hat and gloves and something to keep out the wind such as a showerproof jacket. Your waterproof would do but they can be sweaty and uncomfortable. Always carry an extra sweater.

(7) In all seasons I suggest a long sleeved cotton shirt which opens all down the front. You can wear it open or buttoned to various degrees, or not at all, with sleeves rolled up or down, inside or outside your trousers, and have ventilation or protection from sun, wind, vegetation, insects, as required.

This is general advice based mainly on ordinary clothing. Visit a good outdoor equipment shop and see if they have anything to offer which would improve your comfort. For example, windproof garments and magic vests which do not stay wet like cotton T shirts. First though, try ordinary clothes to find out whether and how they could be improved upon.

I recomend that you carry a compass - and know how to use it.

Using Daywalks

Once you have decided from the General Map (Pages (3) & (4) which routes you want to walk:

* Decide where you want to start and look it up in the list of Junction and Starting Points; use your OS map to get there.

* Jot down a list of your chosen routes in order. The paragraphs of directions are numbered in one direction and lettered in another.
Eg Furnace Mill 20(a), 19(a) & 7(1)

Each route description ends with a note of the route options available to you from the end.

Amendment Service

The countryside changes all the time. You will meet new tracks, stiles, gates and barns; hedges vanish, paths are diverted and trees fall down. To keep directions up to date I issue amendment slips.

IF you write to tell me of any changes or problems that you meet, stating route and paragraph number, I will refund your postage.

IF you send me a stamped addressed envelope with a note of what publication(s) you have, I will send you up to date amendment slips.

John Roberts

Rights of Way & Obstructions

DaywalkS routes are on public rights of way or well established paths and tracks. They may be Foot -paths, Bridleways or Byways (usually green lanes or tracks) with some stretches of ordinary road. Your rights as pedestrian are the same on all, you are entitled to follow the track or cross the land. The fact that it is "private" land (most land is) is quite irrelevant.

Occupiers of land are legally obliged not to obstruct paths, it is an offence, but sometimes they do. Paths should not be ploughed up nor have crops growing over them, nor should you meet barbed wire fences. You are entitled to cross or remove any such obstacles doing as little damage as you reasonably can. You may diverge to pass the obstacle so long as you go no further than is necessary and do not enter someone else's land.

I do not want to give the impression that most paths are blocked solid, they are not. But in a day's walking you may meet a couple of obstacles. I have reported all problems on these routes to the County Councils for attention. If you should meet any please write to me.

The Ramblers Association and other more local footpath and amenity groups have an important role in keeping footpaths open. The RA has Footpath Secretaries for each area who monitor the state of paths, respond to closure and diversion proposals and organise maintenance. If you use footpaths it seems right that you should support them. Use the application form on page (ii) to join.

Junctions & Starting Points

These notes will help you find the start of your walk. Once there you can follow the directions and will not need this list again.

The places are listed alpahbetically. The names are those of the nearest place to the junction that has a name which may be at some distance. In a village it may not be at the centre.

Some Junction Points are the corners of fields or tops of hills and only accessible on foot. I tell you which they are. You can't start there but they are places from which you have a choice of routes.

Directions just after some Starting Points may seem repetitive, pedantic or just plain odd to people already on a route. This is to cater for people joining the route at that spot, to whom I can't say "Go L" untill they are facing the right way.

You will also see in some places messages in capitals eg; ROUTE 8 RUNS L BETWEEN POSTS. The top ends of Routes 8 & 9 illustrate what this is for. They approach Coppicegate on the same track and coming from Arley you might want to go on to Kingswood without visiting Coppicegate. If you do not need information, ignore it.

Each Starting Point is described so you can recognise it when you arrive and a six digit map reference given so you can pinpoint the spot on a map and use the roads to get there. (Map references are not absolutely precise and may be a hundred yards or so out, hence the extra description.) The OS maps show you how to use them.

Arley (SO 767802) stile on bend of lane W of village on River Severn, just W of A442 Kidderminster - Bridgnorth road. Car park, WC's, shops, pubs. Steel footbridge only over river.

Bewdley (SO 787753) town on River Severn W of Kidderminster. All facilities and roadbridge.

Billingsley (SO 714843) pub in straggling hamlet on B4363 S of Bridgnorth. Limited car space.

Birchen Park (SO 705803) point in a wood where four tracks cross. No road access, start elsewhere.

Buttonoak (SO 752780) pub on B4194 W of Bewdley. Shop. Car space 300 yds W in forest.

Burnt Wood (SO 759735) T junctiom of paths near edge of wood. No road access but car space on lane .25 mile W.

Callow Hill (SO 743739) chapel sign W of pub on A456 W of Bewdley and just E of junction of that road with A4117. Some car space.

Chorley Covert (SO 721766) footbridge in dingle S of Billingsley. No road access, start elsewhere.

Coppicegate (SO 729803) small wooden gate at corner of a wood on top of a hill. No road access.

Dowles (SO 780764) footbridge over Dowles Brook where it meets Severn by old bridge piers. Near B4194, no parking, use for drop or pick up.

Furnace Mill (SO 721766) road bridge over Dowles Brook. No parking , use for drop or pick up.

Goodmoorhill (SO 730762) footbridge over Dowles Brook near S edge of Wyre Forest. No road access, start elsewhere.

Gorst Hill (SO 738729) top corner of field with stile. No road access, start elsewhere.

Highley (SO 740833) stile in field corner (find church on S side of village & take path on W side, then pass house on your R to stile). Pubs & shops. Park at a distance.

Kingswood (SO 730769) bend of track by cottage on edge of forest clearing. No road access, start elsewhere.

Kinlet (SO 728802) pub in hamlet on B4363 S from Bridgnorth. Car space.

Knowles Mill (SO 762766) track by Dowles Brook opposite footbridge and water mill. No road access, start elsewhere.

Severn Lodge (SO 753810) stone bridge carries SVRly 150 yds from Severn. No road access.

Watertower (SO 758743) driveway meets A456 by water tower W of Bewdley. No parking, use for drop or pick up.

Woodhill (SO 731842) stile on bend of hedged footpath NW of Highley. Spur path runs to pub and road. Some parking.

List of Routes

All routes are described in both directions, so Route (1) could equally be called "Woodhill - Coppicegate".

You can use the west bank of the River Severn to provide extra circuits, shown by dotted lines on the maps as routes (A) and (B). They are not described in detail since no one ever got lost following the River Severn, but I do tell you what to look for to know when you have arrived at, for example, Severn Lodge.

	Route	Miles	Kms
1	Coppicegate - Woodhill	5	8
2	Woodhill - Chorley Covert (via Billingsley)	3	5
3	Chorley Covert - Woodhill (southern route)	1.75	2.8
4	Chorley Covert - Birchen Park	3	5
5	Birchen Park - Coppicegate	1.75	2.8
6	Birchen Park - Furnace Mill	4.25	6.75
7	Goodmoorhill - Furnace Mill	.75	1.25
8	Coppicegate - Kingswood	2.5	4
9	Coppicegate - Arley	2.5	4
10	Arley - Buttonoak	1.6	2.5
11	Buttonoak - Knowles Mill	1.5	2.5
12	Buttonoak - Kingswood	1.86	3
13	Goodmoorhill - Kingswood	.6	1
14	Goodmoorhill - Knowles Mill	2.8	4.5
15	Bewdley - Knowles Mill	2.6	4.25
16	Burnt Wood - Knowles Mill	2.6	4.2

17	Bewdley - Burnt Wood	2.8	4.5
18	Gorst Hill - Burnt Wood	3	4.8
19	Goodmoorhill - Gorst Hill	3	4.8
20	Gorst Hill - Furnace Mill	4.4	7.25
(A)	River Severn: Severn Lodge - Arley	1.25	2
(B)	River Severn: Arley - Dowles	3.7	6

Sample Circuits

Start	Routes	Miles	Kms
Buttonoak	11-14-13-12	5.5	9
Arley	10-11-15-B	8	13
Bewdley	15-16-17	7.5	12
Buttonoak	12-13-19-18-16-11	11	17
Highley	1-2-4-6-7-13-8-1	16	26
Burnt Wood	18-20-7-13-12-11-16	13	21
Bewdley	Outer Circle	26	42

"Walking in winter - Route 3 near Chorley Covert"

SEVERN VALLEY RAILWAY: The original enterprise
lasted from 1858 to 1963 as a route from Hartelbury
on the main Worcester to Birmingham line up the
River Severn to Shrewsbury. It was independent
until absorbed by the Great Western Railway in
1870.   And allthough the line between Bewdley and
Kidderminster looks a natural part of the original
route it was added only in 1878.   The new link
brought some industrial traffic from the West
Midlands but by and large the line carried
agricultural freight and coal from mines in the
Highley area. This ceased in 1960 and the line got
the Beeching chop in 1963.

The SVR Society was formed in 1965 and by valient
work in both fund raising and engineering, they
were able to reopen the line between Bridgnorth and
Hampton Loade in 1970 and the full stretch to
Bewdley in 1974.   The link with Kidderminster was
restored in 1984.

The are stations at Kidderminster, Bewdley, Arley,
Highley, Hampton Loade and Bridgnorth, all
restored and painted in GWR colours, with old
posters, milk churns, adverts and piles of luggage.
Kidderminster Station is actually new but a well
made replica in turn of the century GWR style. The
sixteen mile trip includes 5 viaducts, two tunnels
and the beautiful Victoria bridge over the Severn
by Trimpley Reservoir. When built in 1861 it was
the biggest cast iron span in the world.

The coaches are painted in the liveries of GWR
(chocolate and cream), LNER (teak), LMS (crimson
lake) and early BR (carmine and cream) by a range
of finely restored steam engines.   This is all
delightful nostaligia, but best of all, the
wonderful scenery is not, it is there now, a real
working landscape which you can really walk.

"Arley Station – steam nostalgia"

"Cart shed & barn - Route 10 near Pound Green"

Main Map Symbols

Starting point	●
Path	..·˙·..
Track	- - ⁻ ⌄ ⌄
Road/lane	∿
Railway	┼┼┼┼┼┼┼┼
Canal	┬┬┬┬┬
Stream	∼⌄∼⌄∼
Rivers, lakes & ponds	≈≈≈
Church	+
Building	■
Car park	□

Map scale - appx 1.5 ins/mile

1 Coppicegate - Woodhill
5 miles   8 kms

There is no Wyre Forest on this route, but there are views across miles of treetops stretching up the valleys. The ends of the route are both quite high and the walk between involves plunging down to the Severn then up again. You walk along the river near the railway and may see a steam train. There is a slightly spooky dingle, climbs up steep grassy fields with nice views and the trace of an old green lane. Near Highley things are more urban.

✳
Coppicegate to Woodhill

(1) At small wooden gate on corner of wood, put wood on your L (repeat - on your L) & FOLLOW WOOD EDGE to field corner.

(2) Go R on field edge track to next field. Go L along hedge to lane.

(3) Go L down to L bend & take track R.

(4) When track ends, keep same line with hedge on you L to where hedge bends R by trees. Go L under trees & cross fence on its corner.

(5) Go R on field edge, pass gate & house R to corner & cross wooden fence.

(6) Cross field diagonally & join track to farm. Go R & take 1st gate L.

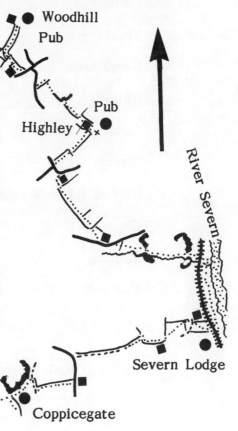

Woodhill Pub

Pub

Highley

River Severn

Severn Lodge

Coppicegate

1

(7) Go downfield diagonally & cross bottom corner fence. (IF OBSTRUCTED try wooden fence half way down R hedge.) Go under rail bridge to Severn.

Severn Lodge

>> OPTIONS <<
Route 1 (para 8 below)
or River Severn Route (A)

(8) From bank of Severn opposite stone railway bridge, go UPSTREAM one field & cross iron bridge.

(9) Go ahead a few paces to pass 1st ruin, then L to follow brook under ·bridge.

(10) Follow line of brook via stile (1) thro dingle to take stile (2).

(11) Here keep same line over field to take stile (3), then R to stile (4) & B4555.

(12) Go L, pass house R & take stile R. Go up & take gate, bear R to next gate, then with fence on your L to take stile.

(13) Keep same line along trees (old track) to houses & onto lane.

(14) Go L to just past L bend & by post box take stile R.

(15) Follow stiles to top R field corner & take stile. Go on a few paces to Springfield House.

Highley

(16) Face Springfield House & take path on its R side. Take stile (1) & on to stile (2) into field.

(17) Go R along hedge to corner. Keep same line with hedge on your L to take field corner stile.

(18) At road, go ahead & take 1st L, then R. Go on to end.

(19) Take FP, bearing L & take stile to sports field. Go L down edge to stile & lane.

(20) Go R to cross roads. Go L & take metal gates R into farm.

(21) Pass sheds on your L, take gate to field. Keep same line on field edge to take corner gate. Go on appx 100 yds to stile L.

ROUTES 2 & 3 GO OVER STILE
CARRY ON BELOW FOR PUB.

(22) Continue up path to Malt Shovel Pub at

Woodhill. ●

>> OPTIONS <<
Routes 2(1) & 3(a)

1

(a) At Malt Shovel Pub, take path on L side of outbuilding. Go down to L bend with stile R,

ROUTES 2 & 3 GO R OVER STILE

(b) At stile between field & footpath, get onto path side. Put your back to stile, go R appx 100 yds & take stile into field.

(c) Go with hedge on your L, take gate & thro farm to lane. Go L to cross roads.

(d) Go R, pass sports field gate, take stile L. Go with hedge on your R & take stile R.

(e) Go L, bearing R to join end of road. Follow it to near end & take road L then R to corner. Take fenced path by last house to field.

(f) Sight church & go to it along hedge. At field corner keep same line appx 100 yds & take corner stile L.

(g) Follow field edge to take stile & pass house to path junction at

Highley.

(h) Face Springfield House then go L & take stile to field.

(i) Go downfield with hedge on your L. Take stile & with hedge on your R to lane.

(j) Go L past lane R to L bend. Take track past houses etc to take stile.

(k) Follow line of trees .25 mile to take stile & on to take gate.

(l) Sight farm below & bear R to take gate & come downfield on R of farm, via stile to B4555.

(m) Go L past house & appx 100 yds to take stile R.

(n) Bear L, take stile then follow line of brook appx .6 mile via stiles to Severn.

(o) Go R, cross iron bridge & follow river to field end. Go R stone rail bridge.

Severn Lodge

>> OPTIONS <<
Route 1 (para p below)
or River Severn Route (A)

(p) At stone railway bridge get on side away from river. Put your back to bridge & go immediately R over fence into field corner.

(q) Go up diagonally to gate & track. Go R, pass gate L & take track opposite farm to field.

(r) Cross diagonally to house & cross wooden fence on its R. Go with fence/hedge on your L past house & gate, to where fences meet under tree.

(s) Cross fence & go with hedge on your R to join track to lane.

(t) Go L to house L. Take track opposite to field corner.

1 (u) Go R to next field corner, then L with wood on your R to small wooden gate.

Coppicegate ●

>> OPTIONS <<
Routes 5(a), 8(1) & 9(1)

2   Woodhill - Chorley Covert
(north via Billingsley)
3 miles   5 kms

With fine views of the Clee Hills to the west, this is a walk of hedgerows and coverts.   There is a prickly path through Hook Plantation. The contours are steep and varied and the whole landscape remote and rural.

✱

Woodhill to Chorley Covert
(north via Billingsley)

(1) At Malt Shovel Pub take path on L of outbuilding down to L bend with stile R.

ROUTE 1 RUNS AHEAD

(2) At stile between field & path, get into field & put your back to stile.

(3) Go R on field edge to take gate/stile.   Bear R to far R field corner.

(4) Cross   dingle   (wire   net enclosure L) & take gate/stile. Go with hedge on your R for 3 fields. Take stile R then with hedge on your L to gate & track.

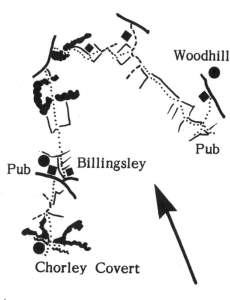

Woodhill

Pub

Pub Billingsley

Chorley Covert

(22)

(5) Go ahead to round R bend & on a few paces. Go L & take 1st gate into field.

(6) Cross to lower R corner & take bridge R. Follow track, at junction go L to field.

(7) Go to just L of barns then L to take gate. Go R to pass barns on your R & along field edge to corner.

(8) Go L appx 100 yds to pass lone rowan tree, then R into dingle. Take easiest route thro, over stream & into far field.

(9) Go L up hedge to lane. Go L, cross bridge & take 1st gate L. Go with fence on your L & take gate into wood.

(10) Go STRAIGHT thro, slight jink L round blockage, to field.

2

(11) Keep same line .2 mile; go thro wide hedge gap, via (? bust) gate, & go ahead to take gate.

(12) Go with hedge on your R to field corner, aim for L end of skyline house. Take take gate R, then UP with hedge on your R, to take stile.

(13) Exit past house to road & on to B4363 at

Billingsley.

(14) Take stile opposite pub & cross field to join L hedge at projecting corner. Go down to track & take stile L.

(15) Go down, pass power pole with gizmo to next pole. Bear L on old track, curving R to bridge.

Chorley Covert

>> OPTIONS <<
Routes 3 (1) & 4(1)

Chorley Covert to Woodhill
(north via Billingsley)

(a) At bridge over stream, get on woodlandside. Go up, parallel with L fence, pass power pole with gizmo & take field top stile to track.

(b) Go R along hedge to its corner, then keep same line to stile & pub at

Billingsley.

(c) Face front of pub then go R & take 1st L. Enter gate of 2nd house (Cheslyn) & pass to take stile.

(d) Go down to take stile then on to field corner & take gate R. Keep same line with hedge on your L to take gate.

(e) Cross & take gate opposite, then keep same line at same level appx .2 mile to wood. Enter at old posts.

(23)

2

(f) Take straight line thro, slight jink R round blockage, & exit at gate. Go with fence on your R to gate & lane.

(g) Go R, cross bridge & up to take 1st gate/gap R. Go 60 paces down field edge.

(h) Enter dingle & go through to field. (Fallen tree problem here but path bears L to cross stream, goes ahead a few paces, then bears L again.)

(i) Go L, round field corner & along edge to barns.

(j) Pass barns on your L & take gate L. Double back into field & bear R to gate & track.

(k) Follow, at junction go R, cross bridge to field. Go L to far field corner gate & track.

(l) Go R, round L bend, & take 1st gate ahead where track bends R.

(m) Go with hedge on your R to take stile R, then on your L for 3 fields to take gate/stile. Pass wire netting enclosure R.

(n) Enter field & bear R to take gate/stile in mid facing hedge.

(o) Go with hedge on your L to stile L.

     ROUTE 3 RUNS R TO
     PROJECTING HEDGE CORNER
(p) Cross stile

     ROUTE 1 RUNS R TO STILE
(q) Go L up hedge path to pub.

Woodhill
>> OPTIONS <<
Routes 1(a) & 3(a)

"Cape of Good Hope - Billingsley"

3 Chorley Covert - Woodhill
(southern route)
1.7 miles   2.75 kms

An exploration of a long dense dingle, rich in birds and wild flowers. See if you can spot the mellowing remnants of a coal industry, there are plenty about. It can be muddy underfoot but the way it perfectly clear, unlike most other dingles in the county. Towards Woodhill you rise sharply out of the valley of the Borle Brook to the high ridge before the Severn Valley. There is a spur from the junction with Routes 1 and 2 to the Malt Shovel pub, which I thought might be appreciated.

Chorley Covert to Woodhill
(southern route)

(1) At bridge, get on woodland side of stream. Put your back to bridge & go R to take small gate into wood.

(2) Follow path appx .4 mile to road. Go R, pass road R & take gate L just before bridge.

(3) Enter open area & go R on path appx 1 mile: (at blockage skirt L round it & rejoin), to path fork.

(4) Go R, cross bridge & curve up L to take stile to lane.

(5) Go L a few paces & take stile up to field. Cross corner & go R on field edge. As it bends L, take hedged path L to stile & field.

(6) Go with hedge on your R via stile/gate, thro old quarry to hedge corner. Cross to stile.

ROUTE 2 RUNS L UP FIELD EDGE

(7) Cross stile.

ROUTE 1 RUNS R DOWN PATH

(8) Go L up to Malt Shovel Inn.

Woodhill
>> OPTIONS <<
Routes 1(a) & 2(1)

3 Woodhill to Chorley Covert
(southern route)

(a) At Malt Shovel Inn take path L of pub down to L bend & stile R.

ROUTE 1 RUNS ON DOWN PATH

(b) Take stile.

ROUTE 2 RUNS R UP FIELD EDGE

(c) With stile at your back, go ahead to projecting hedge corner. Go with hedge on your L thro old quarry, via stile by gate to bottom field corner.

(d) Take stile L & follow hedged path to field. Go R to field corner, but 5 yds from it cross L & take hedge gap to stile & lane.

(e) Go L few paces, take stile & go down to cross bridge.

(f) Go L on MAIN path, ignore small path L, & on to meet path from R.

(g) Take path L appx 1 mile: (at blockage skirt round R & rejoin path) to gate & road with bridge L.

(h) Go R, pass road L to steel railings L & take path by them.

(i) Follow woodland path .4 mile & take small gate. Bear L to bridge.

Chorley Covert

>> OPTIONS <<
Routes 2(a) & 4(1)

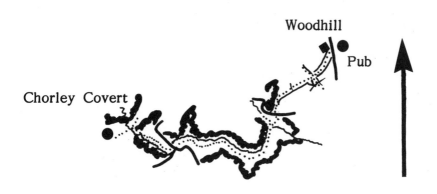

Woodhill

Pub

Chorley Covert

(26)

4

Chorley Covert - Birchen Park
3 miles   5 kms

The chain of small woods on this route were all part of one great forest. Chorley Covert and Bush Wood in the north are mainly oak whilst Gorsty Park and Birchen Park further south are pine and spruce. You can see the difference in the light and life beneath them, thriving creatures and luxuriant plants in the dappled shade of the oaks, and cold beds of grey needles under the conifers.

Chorley Covert

Birchen Park

Chorley Covert to Birchen Park

(1) At bridge over stream get on field (not wood) side. Go up to pass well R of beech. Cross midfield to take midhedge stile.

(2) Go to field corner ahead by wood, take stile & go with wood on your R. Enter wood at corner.

(3) Follow path thro to lane. Go L, pass chapel & take track R.

(4) Pass 2 tracks L & down to cross bridge. Take track L. Just before house take gate L.

(5) Cross open area & back fence onto wood path. Go thro to take stile, then up to ruin.

(6) Pass ruin on your R & take stile, then up to R end of trees on crest & take gate.

(7) Cross summit & down to field corner. Cross fence R, then next fence so wood is on your L.

(8) Go with wood on your L, down (cross fence) & up to take corner gate L.

(9) Follow wood edge 25 yds, take gate R to meet track. Cross, bearing L & take path to track.

(10) Go R, thro gates (1) & (2), then L along fence & via 2 gates to field.

(11) Bear a little L to cross field corner & take gate into wood. Follow wood path, pass broken bridge, to meet track.

(12) Go L. At start of forest road take track L appx .5 mile. After R bend, NB open felled area L, & a few paces on tracks cross.

●

4 Birchen Park
>> OPTIONS <<
Routes 5(1) & 6(1)

Birchen Park to Chorley Covert

✳

(a) Where 4 paths meet in wood, find N route - the one with open felled area on R a few paces from cross tracks.

(b) Follow N route appx .5 mile. After felled area R it bends L & later meets end of forest road.

(c) Keep same line & take 1st path R. Pass broken bridge & follow to take gate into field.

(d) Bear L & take gate jutting into field. Go with fence on your R to wood edge track. Go R & take 1st path L into wood.

(e) Follow to track, cross bearing L, & resume path to gate & field.

(f) Go L & take gate. Go R along fence, down to cross stream & up to field corner.

(g) Cross 2 fences into field R with hill. Cross summit & down to 4 gates.

(h) Take 2nd from L & go down. Make for ruin, take stile, pass ruin on your L, go down into dingle & take stile.

(i) Follow wood path, cross fence. Bear R & take gate to track. Go R, at fork go R up to lane.

(j) Go L, take FP L. Take R of 2 paths into wood & go thro on straight line to exit at wood corner into field.

(k) Follow wood edge, to cross next fence. Leave wood, cross midfield & take midhedge stile. Bear R to beech & down L to bridge

Chorley Covert ●
>> OPTIONS <<
Routes 2(a) & 3(1)

5 Birchen Park - Coppicegate
1.86 miles 3 kms

The village of Kinlet lies in a valley and this
route sweeps down to it then up again. There are
fair views of a hilly landscape with some
parkland on the west side.

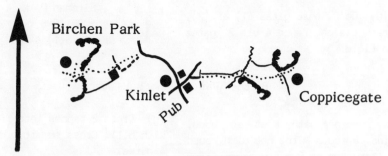

Birchen Park

Kinlet

Pub

Coppicegate

Birchen Park to Coppicegate

*

(1) Where 4 tracks meet in wood,
they go N, S, E & W. (N has open
felled area on R a few paces on.)

(2) Take E track to wood edge
gate. Cross & go to nearest oak.

(3) Sight past next oak to power
pole with gizmo. Take this line
to projecting fence corner.

(4) Pass house etc on your R to
field corner. Cross fence & bear
R to bottom field corner. Join
track & go on to lane.

(5) Go R to B4363 at

Kinlet.

(6) Pass pub on your R & go appx
150 yds to take next road R. Take
end gate.

(7) Go with hedge on your L into
wood, & thro to take gate.

(8) Go up midfield with trees each
side. Keep same line to meet small
wooden gate in top hedge.

Coppicegate
>> OPTIONS <<
Routes 1(1), 8(1) & 9(1)

5 Coppicegate to Birchen Park

*

(a) At small wooden gate by wood corner put your back to gate so wood is on R. (Check: back to gate wood on your R.)

(b) Go down midfield & take white field bottom gate into wood.

(c) Follow wood path then field edge to B4363. Go L to pub at

Kinlet.

(d) From T junction take drive past lodge appx .4 mile & take track L.

(e) Go a few paces & take gate R. Make for top of field just R of farm & cross fence.

(f) Go with fence on your L to its corner.

(g) Sight ahead on same line two oaks & make for them.

(h) Pass oaks on your R then bear R to take wood edge gate.   Follow wood path to cross tracks.

Birchen Park
●

>> OPTIONS <<
Routes 4(a) & 6(1)

"Oaks in winter - Kinlet Park, Route 5"

6

Birchen Park - Furnace Mill
4.25 miles   6.75 kms

In the north you pass through dark mysterious conifers but are soon in the open, along upper edge of a valley through a pastoral landscape.

Next comes a wonderful walk through oaks. There are conifers but maturing and more widely spaced. Much of the route is on the forest edge, a good place to watch for deer, tread lightly, breathe softly.

The sweeping grassy ride is part of the Elan Valley aquaduct. It carries pure soft lake water seventy miles from Mid Wales to Birmingham, plunging down valleys and shooting up hills, and without ever a pump.

* Birchen Park to Furnace Mill

(1) At cross tracks in forest, routes go N, S, E & W. N has open area on R a few paces on. Take S track to lane.

(2) Go L appx .25 mile, pass house & take next gate R. Cross field diagonally to join far edge. Follow it to house & B4363.

(3) Go R past house & a few paces on, take stile L.

(4) Bear R to join R hedge & follow .4 mile to round field corner & take next gate R.

(5) Go ahead along tree row to take gate & enter wood. Follow track to junction.

(6) Go L a few paces to gate, then take wood edge path .4 mile, via stile, to junction.

(7) Bear L & follow wood edge path, becomes grass track & leaves wood edge, appx .75 mile. Cross grass ride with brick thingy L, to forest road.

(8) Go L to gate & lane. Go ahead appx .4 mile to track R. DON'T TAKE IT.

ROUTE 20 RUNS DOWN TRACK

(9) Keep on lane, pass lane L, to bridge.

Furnace Mill
●

>> OPTIONS <<
Routes 7(a) & 20(a)

6

Furnace Mill to Birchen Park

(a) At bridge brook flows W to E. Get road N pass lane R to track L.

ROUTE 20 RUNS DOWN TRACK

(b) Keeo on road appx .4 mile to R bend & take gate into forest. Follow track, round L bend & go appx 100 paces to take track R.

(c) Follow appx .75 mile; cross grass ride with brick structure R, & on to meet hard track.

(d) Go R along forest edge .4 mile to gate R. DON'T TAKE IT.

(e) Go L a few paces to junction & take track R to take wood edge gate.

(f) Go ahead along tree row & take gate.

(g) Go L, round field corner & go with hedge on your L appx .4 mile.

Birchen Park

Furnace Mill

(h) Nearing end hedge bear R & take mid hedge stile to B4363. Go R, pass house & take next gate L.

(i) Go with hedge on your L till it bends away L, then cross field bearing R to gate & lane.

(j) Go L appx .25 mile & take first gate R into wood. Follow track down to cross tracks.

Birchen Park

>> OPTIONS <<
Routes 4(a) & 5(1)

7

Furnace Mill - Goodmoorhill
.75 miles   1.25 kms

A woodland route following the Dowles Brook. The
eastern part is an easy stroll round the book's
meanders, but to the west is a rocky miniature
gorge. There is one steep tricky part but
it lasts only for a couple of yards.
Go in the bluebell season.

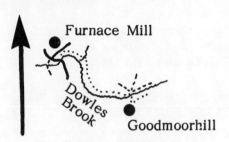

Furnace Mill to Goodmoorhill

(1) At road bridge brook flows S-N
just here. Go N on W bank.

(2) Follow waterside path. Steep
tricky stretch lasts only a few
feet.

Goodmoorhill to Furnace Mill

(a) At footbridge brook runs W to
E. Go W on N bank appx .5 mile.

(3) At tributory path forks, go L
a few paces, then R to cross
tributory.

(b) Cross tributory stream & go L.
A few paces on take R fork.

(4) Keep to waterside path .5
mile, ignoring track L, to
footbridge.

(c) Continue along stream, steep
tricky bit lasts only a few feet,
to road bridge.

Furnace Mill
●

>> OPTIONS <<
Routes 6(a) & 20(a)

Goodmoorhill
●

>> OPTIONS <<
Routes 13(1), 14(1) & 19(1)

DOWLES BROOK: Rising on Wyre Common on high
ground just north east of Cleobury Mortimer,
Dowles Brook winds and twists six miles to the
Severn. Several tributaries come from north and
south, but only three are named. The Baveny Brook
contributes its quota at a secret spot in the
middle of the western block of the forest, the Mad
Brook and Lem Brook join near Furnace Mill.

The brook marks the boundary between Shropshire and
Worcestershire and in the past powered four water
mills. Furnace Mill is now a rather magnificent
private house. Coopers Mill is south from
Buttonoak and serves a magnificent purpose as an
outdoor and field studies centre for youth clubs.
Knowles Mill about a quarter of a mile east of
Coopers seems the most preserved, a modest,
comfortable private house in a pretty setting with
the wheel house still standing opposite. Town Mill,
now a house, is little nearer to the Severn on the
other side of the brook.

"Knowles Mill"
(34)

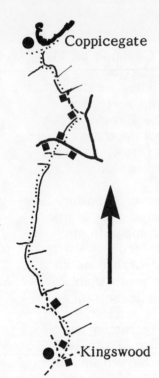

Coppicegate

8

Coppicegate - Kingswood
2.5 miles 4 kms

This hedgerow route is almost a ridge walk which gives a feeling of space and some fine distant views. Strangely, the Wyre is only visible now and then because of the lie of the land. Near Coppicegate is/was a titanic pile of horse manure nearly six feet high, I hope the animal is not out loose. The section near Coppicegate is shared with Route 8.

Kingswood

Coppicegate to Kingswood

(1) At small gate by wood corner, put your back to gate so wood is behind on your R. (Check; wood behind on R.) Go L down field edge & take corner gate/gap.

(2) Go up with hedge on your L to take gap L (or stile if not bust).

(3) Go R on field edge, round field corner, pass house & take fenced path R to track.

(4) Follow almost to lane, to gate of Dormer Cottage R.

ROUTE 9 RUNS AHEAD TO LANE

(5) Go R via concrete posts, 2 fields, to B4194.

(6) Go R appx 150 yds to end of wooden fence L. Take stile L by power pole.

(7) Pass pond on your L, bear half R & cross grass to take stile in opposite fence.

(8) Go ahead midfield & take hedge gap. Keep same line, pass between strawberries, to take hedge gap.

(9) Go with hedge on your L 2 fields, to corner by blue barn R, & cross hedge.

(35)

(10) Go with hedge on your R to take gate. Join track down to take farm gate.

(11) Pass buildings on your L, cross track & on with small paddocks L. At end of their hedge take gate L.

(12) Go with hedge on your R, via gate, to field corner stile R, & take hedged path to track.

(13) Go 15 yds L to junction.

Kingswood
●

8

>> OPTIONS <<
Routes 12(a) & 13(a)

Kingswood to Coppicegate

(a) At track junction by bungalow, stand ON junction with bunaglow on your R. Take track ahead 15 yds then track R.

(b) Follow path to stile & field. Go L with hedge on your L, via 2 gates, to track.

(c) Keep same line, pass farm R & down track past buildings to take gate.

(d) Follow track upfield & take gate. Go with hedge on your L to corner by blue barn L.

(e) Cross hedge ahead & go with hedge on your R, 2 fields, to take field corner gap.

(f) Bear a little R & go midfield between strawberry beds, & thro next hedge gap.

(g) Keep same line midfield to twin poplars in far fence, take stile.

(h) Go ahead, pass L of pond & bear L to stile & B4194.

(i) Go R, pass house L, to open field. Go L with hedge on your L via 2 fields & twin concrete posts to track.

ROUTE 9 RUNS R TO LANE

(j) Go L to track end. Take fenced path on R of house gate to field.

(k) Go L & round field corner with hedge on your L to next corner. Take gap L (or stile if not bust).

(l) Go R with hedge on your R, down field edge to take corner gate/gap R. Go up with hedge on your R to small gate L at wood corner.

●

Coppicegate

>> OPTIONS <<
Routes 1(1), 5(a) & 9(1)

9

Coppicegate - Arley
2.5 miles   4 kms

This route traces a long slope between the Severn at 25 metres and a hilltop at about 134 but it is steep only in the Severn Valley. At either end the views are superb. The central section plunges darkly through the Wyre for about two miles, on forest tracks through conifers. Routes 8 and 9 share the northern half mile.

* Coppicegate to Arley

(1) From small gate on crest near corner of wood, go down with hedge on your L, leaving wood behind. (Repeat: fence on L, wood behind.)

(2) Take gate, go up with hedge on your L & take gap (or stile if not bust) L.

(3) Go R, round field corner & take fenced path L of house. Follow track to lane.

ROUTE 8 RUNS R

(4) Go L appx 100 yds & take track R appx .6 mile to glade.

(5) Make for track leaving far side of glade by bearing L off track & circling behind huts.

(6) Follow earth track, cross forest road (1) to (2). Go L appx .25 mile to hairpin R bend.

(7) Find path L on corner & go down bank to stream. Cross & go L up to lane.

(8) Go R to lane junction. Go R & take 1st gate R. Go with hedge on your L .3 mile to field corner.

(9) Cross to lower field & follow wood edge to its corner. Cross field on same line to far L corner stile, & lane.

ROUTE 10 RUNS R

(10) Go L down to

Arley.

>> OPTIONS <<
Route 10(1) or
River Severn (A) or (B).

9

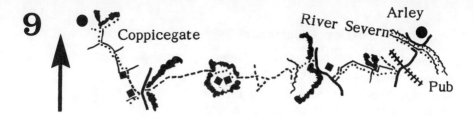

Coppicegate

River Severn

Arley

Pub

The cottages in the clearing at about half
way are not ancient, but most of the clearings in
the Wyre are recorded in the Domesday Book. See
how the chalets are gathered, add some chickens and
swine and smoke from a cooking fire, dress the
weekenders in coarse woolen tunics, turn their
cars into carts and sledges, and there you have it.

✱ Arley to Coppicegate

(a) From river take lane up over
railway to track R with stile on
corner.

ROUTE 10 RUNS L

(b) Take stile & go R to
projecting wood corner, then along
wood edge to upper field corner.

(c) Cross to field above & go with
hedge on your R appx .3 mile to
gate, then L to lane.

(d) Go R appx .2 mile to Hungry
Hill Camp & Caravan sign. Take
path opposite on R of power pole.

(e) Follow path down, pass holy
bush, ignore L fork a few paces
on, to LOWEST point by stream.

(f) Cross & take R fork up to
forest road.

(g) Go R appx .25 mile & take 1st
track R. Cross forest road, reach
glade.

(h) Go R, circle huts & take track
appx .6 mile to lane.

(i) Go L appx 100 yds to L bend &
take track R.

ROUTE 8 RUNS L

(j) Go to track end end & take
fenced path on R of house.

(k) Go L, round field edge to next
field corner. Take gap L (or
stile if not bust).

(l) Go R on field edge, take gate.
Go with hedge on your R to gate R
on crest.

Coppicegate
>> OPTIONS <<
Routes 1(1), 5(a) & 8(1)

Arley - Buttonoak
1.6 miles   2.6 kms

Superb views of the Severn Valley, the
railway, the river and all its hills and
woods, with a stroll through an oakwood.
Pound Green Common is the high point, one
of the ancient clearances in the Wyre. In
summer it is a sea of green bracken,
in autumn a palate of reds and browns.

10

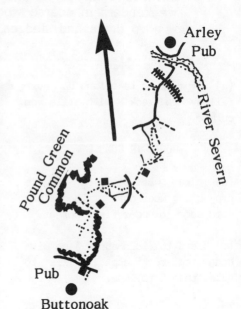

❋ Arley to Buttonoak

(1) From River go up & cross
railway to 1st track R.

ROUTE 9 TAKES STILE ON CORNER

(2) Follow lane up. Pass 1st
track L on bend & go on a few
paces to enter 2nd.

(3) Pass pond R & enter next
field.   Go R off track & Go up
passing midfield oak on your L, to
take far topfield corner stile.

(4) Go up field edge & take gate L
to track. Go R to lane.

(5) Go R appx 50 yds & take 1st
gate L.   Go to far R corner &
cross end hedge with cottage ahead

(6) Go L a few paces then R to
pass brick & stone cottage on your
R. Meet track on garden corner by
railings.

(7) Tracks go L, R & ahead.   Go
ahead midcommon to stone shed. Go
L to join track.

(8) Go L. Watch for wood corner R
& take stile into wood.

(9) Follow path to cross paths, go
L to stile.   DON'T CROSS; take
wood edge path R to B4194.

Buttonoak.
>> OPTIONS <<
Routes 11(1) & 12(1)

10

*

Buttonoak to Arley

(a) Face house opposite pub & take entrance on its L side.

(b) Follow wood edge path to stile. DON'T CROSS. Turn away & follow path to junction.

(c) Go R to stile & track. Go L past house & take 1st path R to stone shed.

(d) Go R to railings & cottage. Keep same line, passing cottage on your L to hedge at edge of common.

(e) Bear L a few paces & find hedge gap into field ahead. Cross to gate & lane.

(f) Go R appx 50 yds & take track L. Ignore R fork. Pass house & go appx 150 yds to take gate L by power pole with gizmo.

(g) Go R down field edge & take corner stile. Cross diagonally, passing midfield oak on your L, & down to corner & track.

(h) Pass pond on your L to lane. Go R to junction with track L.

ROUTE 9 TAKES STILE ON CORNER.

(i) Continue down lane to river

●

Arley

>> OPTIONS <<
Route 9(a) &
River Severn (A) & (B).

11

Buttonoak - Knowles Mill
1.5 miles   2.5 kms

A gradual fall through the oakwoods on forest tracks. Buttonoak is on the edge of a large clearing in the Wyre at a height of about 105 metres. At the bottom is Dowles Brook at 30. Very easy walking.

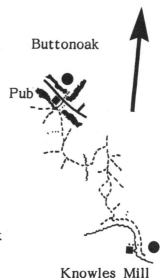

Buttonoak

Pub

Knowles Mill

(1) Face pub & go L to take stile R on 1st field corner.

(2) Go ahead & take stile to wood. Go on a few paces & take 1st track L.

(3) Follow; pass track R & track from L to join track from R. Take next L.

(4) Go on & take next track L, down to cross bridge & up round bends to T junction.

(5) Go R to junction & Coopers Mill sign & keep same track, bearing R.

(6) Pass track R, then tracks L, then track R (!), & down to T junction.

(7) Go L, pass track L, & round R to meet track.

ROUTE 14 RUNS R

(8) Go sharp L along brook, via gate, to bridge & Mill R.

●

Knowles Mill
>> OPTIONS <<
Routes 14a), 15(1) & 16(a)

(a) Stand on track with brook & Mill on your L. Go ahead.

(b) Take gate & on appx 200 yds to meet track.

ROUTE 14 RUNS ON AHEAD

(c) Go sharp R, curve L past 1st track R & take 2nd R.

(d) Follow main track; track from L joins, then tracks from R, then from L, to Coopers Mill sign at junction.

(e) Keep same track, & go on appx 50 yds to take track L.

(f) Follow round bends & over bridge to track junction (1).

(g) Go R to junction (2), go R to junction (3), go R. Pass track R with distant green gate & follow to wide ride.

(h) Take stile R & go with hedge on your R to tale stile to B4194 & pub.

●

Buttonoak
>> OPTIONS <<
Routes 10(a) & 12(1)

I have seen fallow deer in most parts of the Wyre
and the outlying woods, usually in twos and threes.
Once I walked right up to a buck with full antlers
who stood cropping brambles in a ride.

COPPICING is the cutting back young trees to produce sticks and poles. The stumps are left to shoot and will grow a mass of small stems from a stool, which after 15 years or so can be harvested again. The OS map shows how this was organised with the forest divided into areas known as "falls" bearing the names you can see, Oxbind Coppice, Bells Coppice, Gibbonswell Coppice etc.

Coppicing gave fuel for charcoal burning and salt evaporation, palings, stakes, peasticks, baskets, hurdles and firewood. Allthough it has not been carried out on a large scale since the last War you can still see traces. Some trees have several main trunks starting from ground level, others have a single main stem but it starts with a sideways bend as a side shoot grew from the stool. Sometimes enveloping occurs, when a new trunk completely covers the old stool to produce a "false standard". Fungii and disese will have attacked the stool so the tree will not give the timber it promises.

CHARCOAL BURNING: Charcoal for iron smelting was originally made on round flat hearths, shallow excavations in the forest floor about 10 feet in diameter. They are now long overgrown and returned to nature but some are still recognisable. Four foot poles were laid in a dense conical stack, a fire lit at the centre and the stack roofed with turves to exclude air. A big stack might take four or five days to burn up. They needed constant attention because the turf tended to dry and burn and had to be augmented and damped.

Later metal retorts were used, the sides formed by three circular units fiting one above the other and topped with a lid. They had the advantage that air was efficiently excluded without turves and the retort could be left alone to burn.

Buttonoak

Pub

Buttonoak - Kingswood
1.86 miles   3 kms

One third of this route is through mature conifers, one third oaks and the rest open pasture. You meet the Elan Aquaduct from Rhaeder to Birmingham as it falls dramatically into a valley. There is the remnant of an old slightly sunken, slightly obstructed green lane and two remote little stone farm houses.

12

Kingswood

*

Buttonoak to Kingswood

(1) At pub take iron stile on garden (not car park) side of pub.

(2) Go ahead with hedge R & take stile. Follow wide grassy ride appx .6 mile, over crest & track, & down to short post with arrow.

(3) Go L, pass 1st path R & take 2nd R, down to sharp L bend. Go R down to stream.

(4) Cross upfield diagonally to take stile. Follow line of green lane, curving R to take gate.

(5) Pass farms (1) & (2) to cross tracks with bunaglow L.

●
Kingswood
>> OPTIONS <<
Routes 8(a) & 13(a)

* Kingswood to Buttonoak

(a) At T junction of tracks by bungalow, take track to pass bunglalow ON YOUR R.

(b) Pass house & farm (1) & on track to pass farm (2) on your L & take gate.

(c) Go R round field corner & follow obstructed green lane to its end. Take stile.

(d) Cross field diagonally & cross stream. Follow forest path to junction.

(e) Go up L, pass L fork, to wide grassy ride.

(f) Go R appx .6 mile, over crest & track to end. Take stile & go ahead to iron stile & B4194 at

●
Buttonoak.
>> OPTIONS <<
Routes 10(a) & 11(1)

13

Goodmoorhill - Kingswood
.62 miles 1 km

A short link route through the forest which slopes from the valley of the Dowles Brook at about 60 metres to the forest edge at 134. The northern part is oakwood. Splendidly muddy.

Kingswood

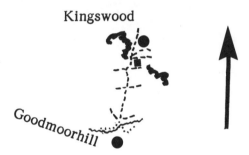

Goodmoorhill

Goodmoorhill to Kingswood

(1) At steel bridge over brook, brook runs W to E. Go N a few paces to cross tracks junction.

(2) Tracks go E, N & NW. Take middle one - N.

(3) Keep same line, crossing 2 tracks to T junction of tracks with bungalow R.

●

Kingswood
>> OPTIONS <<
Routes 8(a) & 12(a)

Kingswood to Goodmoorhill

(a) At T junction of tracks by bungalow, stand ON junction with bungalow behind on your L. Go L into forest.

(b) Follow track over 3 cross tracks to stream & bridge.

●

Goodmoorhill
>> OPTIONS <<
Routes 7(1), 14(1) & 19(1)

This route along the valley of the
Dowles Brook is level and in places
close to the brook, so where it is
not a made up forestry road there may
be mud to enjoy. There are oaks but
the western part is mainly through
conifers, softened near the brook by
birch and beech, with bluebells and
primroses in season.

Goodmoorhill
-
Knowles Mill
2.8 miles   4.5 kms

14

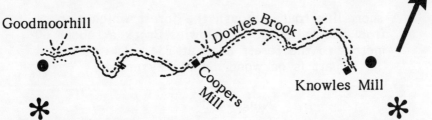

Goodmoorhill

Dowles Brook

Coopers Mill

Knowles Mill

*

Goodmoorhill to Knowles Mill

*

Knowles Mill to Goodmoorhill

(1) At footbridge brook flows W to
E. Go N a few paces & take track R
along brook appx 1.5 miles. Pass
footbridges (1) & (2) R to
junction with pond L.

(2) Pass pond & go R. Cross
bridge & go appx .5 mile to sharp
R bend with horseshoe sign. Keep
same   line ALONG BROOK,   cross
bridge & up to track.

(3) Go R. Pass Coopers Mill to
fork.

ROUTE 11 RUNS UP L

(4) Fork R & on appx .5 mile to
footbridge, house & Mill R.

●

Knowles Mill
>> OPTIONS <<
Routes 11(a), 15(1) & 16(a)

(a) Stand on track with Mill on
your L. Go ahead appx .4 mile,
take gate & on appx 200 yds to
meet track.

ROUTE 11 RUNS UP R

(b) Keep on, pass Coopers Mill L &
take next track L to cross bridge.

(c) Go R along brook, join track &
on appx .7 mile to cross bridge to
junction by pond.

(d) Go L, at next fork go R. Pass
footbridge (1) then appx 1.5 mile,
past footbridge (2) L, to next
footbridge (3) L with track
junction R.

●

Goodmoorhill
>> OPTIONS <<
Routes 7(1), 13(1) & 19(1)

By the Severn near Bewdley watch out for comfrey, with its blue and pink flowers. Watch out for the nature reserves. Where the Dowles Brook joins the Severn you meet the remains of the railway to Cleobury Mortimer and on to join the Hereford - Shrewsbury line at Wooferton. It follows more or less the line of t1e Brook, on embankments or in cuttings, but only the part nearest the Severn is open to the public.

Knowles Mill
- Bewdley

2.6 miles
4.25 kms

15

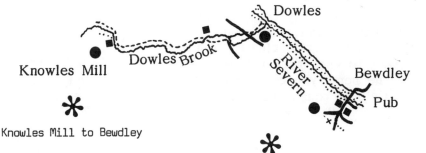

Knowles Mill to Bewdley

(1) Stand on track with Mill on your R. Go ahead appx .5 mile to cross brick bridge.

(2) At next R bend, take gate L by Fred Dale sign, to B4194.

(3) Go R appx 100 yds & take next gate L to Severn.

Dowles
>> OPTIONS <<
Route 15 (below)
or River Severn (B).

(4) At mouth of brook near old bridge piers, go downstream to

●
Bewdley.
>> OPTIONS <<
Route 17(1) or have a beer

Bewdley to Knowles Mill

(a) From road bridge over Severn, go upstream on town side bank .8 mile, to cross iron bridge over brook.

Dowles
>> OPTIONS <<
Route 15 (below) or
River Severn (B).

(b) Go L to B4194. Go R appx 100 yds & just past old bridge take FP L appx .4 mile to lane.

(c) Go R .5 mile to Mill L.

●
Knowles Mill
>> OPTIONS <<
Routes 11(a), 14(a) & 16(a)

16

Burnt Wood - Knowles Mill
2.6 miles 4.2 kms

A varied woodland walk, mainly
through oaks. This routes falls
gently from about 150 metres on
the southern edge of the Wyre to
about 30 at the Dowles Brook. There
are few views but a series of
features - gently rising pasture,
the water tower, the woodland homes
and a wide ride cleared of tall
trees to encourage wildlife. In
the north you cross a thistly
field of rough grazing edged
with sloe trees.

Burnt Wood to Knowles Mill

(1) At paths on edge of wood, face
into wood. Take path L appx 22
paces & take path L.

(2) Follow round edge of wood to
exit at stile. Go with hedge on
your L, via 2 stiles & take stile
to track. Go L to A4117.

Watertower

(3) Put your back to tower facing
road & go L, past row of houses &
take next lane R. Follow, becomes
track, pass track R, to last house
R & take gate/gap ahead.

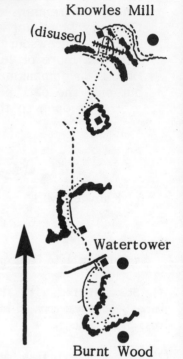

Knowles Mill

(disused)

Watertower

Burnt Wood

(4) Follow wood edge track,
bending R to junction by
Conservancy sign.

(5) Go L down wide ride, ignore
faint track R, to junction. Go R,
pass 2 faint tracks R then curve R
past corner of fence R (round open
land). Go on appx 50 yds to track
junction.

(6) Go L, pass 3 faint tracks R, to main cross track. Take track opposite to next cross track.

(7) Go L appx 24 paces, cross track & go ahead to take stile.

(8) Go down midfield to cross old rail bridge, & on to take stile to track by house.

16

Knowles Mill to Burnt Wood

(a) At track by Mill, cross bridge to Mill & follow path up R.

(b) Pas gate R & with fence on your R to take stile R.

(c) Go down a few paces then fork L on field path. Take field top stile to track by house.

(d) Cross track & take stile. Cross rail bridge & follow field path up to take stile into wood.

(e) Go ahead a few paces & cross track, then appx 24 paces to small cross path. Go R to meet track.

(f) Cross & take path opposite (bearing L). Ignore 2 faint tracks R, to fence round open land.

(g) Go R on path, pass fence corner, ignore 2 faint tracks L & join track.

(9) Go R, take stile, bear L & take stile to wood.

(10) Go L with fence on your L & follow path down, thro houses & cross bridge to track.

●

Knowles Mill
>> OPTIONS <<
Routes 11(a), 14(a) & 15(1)

(h) Keep appx same line, ignore faint track L, to Conservancy sign on wood edge.

(i) Go R on path with wood edge fence on your L & take gate/gap to track.

(j) Follow to A4117. Go L appx 50 yds to "Tarn" sign.

Watertower

(k) Take track by tower to end of hedge R, then bear R to take stile by gate.

(l) Go with hedge on your R, via 2 stiles, & take stile into wood.

(m) Follow path round wood edge to meet path. Go R appx 22 paces to meet path on wood edge.

●

Burnt Wood
>> OPTIONS <<
Routes 17(a) & 18(a)

THE BEWDLEY TO LEOMINSTER RAILWAY: Built
by the Severn Valley Railway in 1861, the line
crossed the Severn a few yards north of Dowles
Brook. A tinted photograpgh of 1864 which can be
bought from the Bewdley Museum shows a train

crossing the new steel decked bridge. The brick and
stone piers are still in place and you can trace
the trackbed westward through the forest by a
succession of cuttings and embankments. You will
have to do some of your tracing on the map because
some parts are open to the public.

The line followed the valley of Dowles Brook to
the old Wyre Forest Station, just south of
Furnace Mill, then turned south to a junction at
Blount Arms near Cleobury Mortimer. A spur ran to
Ditton Priors north of Brown Clee Hill via
Stottesdon, Aston Botterell and Cleobury North, a
railway apparently trying to get away from it all
and commit commercial suicide. In fact it served a
naval amunition dump so the seclusion was
reasonable.

From Blount Arms the main line continued via Neen
Sollars, Newnham Bridge and Tenbury Wells to
Woofferton (that's right), where it joined the main
Hereford to Shrewsbury line. What a wistful, rural
idyll, that vision of pastoral England from the
Flanders and Swann song "The Slow Train". Not
surprisingly it never made money, but good heavens,
who cares, perhaps God never intended it to. The
unsympathetic Dr Beeching did not hear or did not
understand this approach and so the line was
closed in 1961 and the track raised a couple of
years later.

OAKS: The Pedunculate or English Oak (Quercus robur) thrives in damp alkaline soils. Recognise it by its short leaf stems but long acorn stalks. Branches often form a sucession of dog legs creating a massive round dome about 60 feet high.

The Durmast or Sessile Oak (Quercus petraea) prefers drier more acid conditions. Its leaf stalks are long but its acorn stalks short. The branches do not grow in zig zags so the overall form of the tree tends to be tall and straight.

In the Wyre we have both varieties. The English Oak occupies valley bottoms where limey deposits have been leached out from higher ground. The Durmast grows on the valley sides and hilltops which tend to be gravely and sandy and well drained. Its contribution to the plant and animal habitat is less rich.

"Formicus Rufus lives here - ants nest on Route 12"

17

Bewdley - Burnt Wood
2.8 miles   4.5 kms

The Worcestershire landscape at its best, steep
little hills, miles of treetops, a deep dingle and
an airy oakwood. The routes rises from the River
Severn at about 30 metres and travels up a long
shoulder to about 160.   Watch for the massive
spreading beech in Rock Coppice.

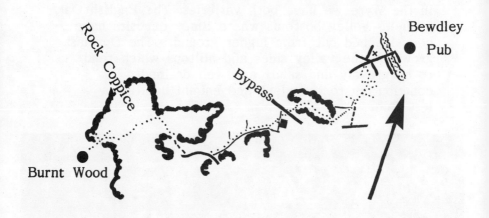

Bewdley to Burnt Wood

✳

(1) From central church, take Park
Lane (above it). Pass Almshouses
L & take path just after.

(2) Take gate, ignore R fork & go
appx .3 mile; pass pond R & cross
field, to join track by gate R.
(DON'T TAKE IT.)

(3) Pass gate & bear R onto field.
Go up to top corner & take stile.

(4) Go down R to cross stream. Go
L with stream on your L. When
path RISES UP R from stream, go
down L & cross it.

(5) Go R across tributory, take
path up to wood edge. Go ahead on
faint paths to cross bypass & TAKE
STEPS. (In case you go wrong; find
steps, NOT path by bridge.)

(6) Go R appx 100 yds & take stile L. Bear R over field & take stile. Go L, pass house & meet cross path with stile L. (DON'T TAKE IT.)

(7) Go R midfield to wood corner. Go with wood (then hedge) on your L keep same line .5 mile to lane.

(8) Go R appx .25 mile to L bend. Take track R to wood.

(9) Just inside go L a few paces, then follow path .16 mile to path junction at corner of wood. ◀

(10) Face this corner, then take track L (NOT along wood edge). Follow appx .4 mile;
 - ignore faint path R,
 - ignore clear one L,
 - at next fork (tree has white mark) go L,
 - at sign, join wood edge path
 - go R to meet path.

(11) Go L to wood edge with path R

●

17 Burnt Wood
>> OPTIONS <<
Routes 16(1) & 18(a)

✱ Burnt Wood to Bewdley

(a) At path junction on wood edge, put your back to wood edge, go ahead 30 paces then take path R.

(b) Follow appx .4 mile to path junction on recessed wood corner.

(c) CARE; stand at end of path you came on, turn R & take 2nd path R.

(d) Follow .3 mile, path leaves wood, joins track, to lane bend.

(e) Go L .25 mile & enter wood. At 1st R bend, go L onto path.

(f) Go R along wood edge. Keep same line appx .5 mile, with wood/hedge/fence on your R, to far end of a wood. ◀

(g) Cross midfield to meet path & stile ahead (DON'T TAKE IT.) Go L, pass house on your R & take stile.

(h) Pass house gate & take stile R. Bear L & take stile to bypass.

(i) Go R appx 100 yds to take steps & cross road. Go straight ahead on path into tip of wood.

(j) Go down into dingle, cross small stream, then big one. Go R, down valley to pond & fence.

(k) Go R over stream & up L to take stile L. Go down to far L field corner & track.

(1) Go L into ●

Bewdley
>> OPTIONS <<
Route 15(a) or home for tea

Gorst Hill - Burnt Wood
3 miles   4.75 kms

There are two great steep grassy valleys, a ridgewalk, two dingles, and a passage through old orchards. It is all rurally remote and magnificent.

18

*

Gorst Hill

Gorst Hill to Burnt Wood

(1) At top corner of field, go down with hedge on your R to stream, & cross bridge.

(2) Go R along stream to hedge, then up with hedge on your R to gate.

(3) Go ahead parallel with fence on your L to gate & lane.

(4) Go L & just before R bend take double gates R into farm.

(5) Cross yard & take path L to field. Go with fence on your L, pass gate L a few paces & take stile L near corner of next field.

(6) Go down with fence on your L, then R round bottom corner to cross stream L.

(7) Take stile & go up.   CARE; when bank L falls away, a fence starts & field L has small enclosure.

(8) Cross fence & enclosure & next fence. Go up midfield via gate (1) & gate (2) to lane.

(9) Go L to junction then R to take track L.

(10) Pass ruin & take stile R. Cross next stile & keep same line appx .3 mile; via gates, to pass L of farm & down to stream.

(11) Follow track up to lane. Go L a few paces & take lane R.

(12) Pass office & take path L before greenhouse. Enter wood edge a few paces to path L.

●

Burnt Wood
>> OPTIONS <<
Routes 16(1) & 17(a)

✳

(a) At path junction on wood edge, go out of wood to lane.

(b) Go R to lane. Go L a few paces & take 1st track R down to cross stream.

(c) Go up & take gate on R of house. Keep same line appx .3 mile; via 2 gates, then midfield & via stiles to track.

(d) Go L to lane, go R to junction then L to entrance R.

(e) Take gate on L of drive. Go down midfield, take gate & keep same line to bottom. Cross fence (1), small wet patch, & fence (2) to path.

(f) Go R & cross stream into field. Go R, round field corner & up with fence on your R to take top corner stile.

(g) Go R with hedge/fence on your R to approach farm, then R to yard & lane.

(h) Go L, pass farm R & take 1st gate R. Go parallel with R fence & take midhedge gate.

(i) Go down with hedge on your L to stream. Go R, cross bridge, & go upfield with hedge on your L to top corner.

●

Gorst Hill
>> OPTIONS <<
Routes 19(a) & 20(1)

"Waterway - Route 12 at Buttonoak"

19

Goodmoorhill - Gorst Hill
3 miles 4.75 kms

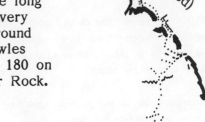

A sequence of small patches of oakwood and pasture with one long woodland section which is very varied and beautiful. The ground rises steadily from the Dowles Brook at 30 metres to about 180 on the steep grassy contours near Rock.

Goodmoorhill to Gorst Hill

(1) Brook runs W to E. Go S & cross bridge. Ignore 2nd bridge R & go up L to stile & track.

(2) Cross bridge, join lane & go appx .25 mile to junction with lane L.

(3) Go L, take 1st stile R. Go down field edge & take stiles (1) & (2) to field.

(4) Go R with wood on your R & take field end gate. Follow track appx 100 yds & take next stile L.

(5) Go a few paces, take stile R, then down with fence on your L to cross bridge & stile.

(6) Go L, round corner & up wood edge to take stile.

(7) Take marked path R, bends R then L, crosses track, & on to stile & track.

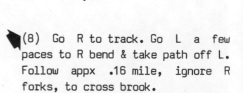

(8) Go R to track. Go L a few paces to R bend & take path off L. Follow appx .16 mile, ignore R forks, to cross brook.

(9) Follow path up, it levels, ignore FAINT path R, to clear junction with path R, by tree marked "56". (Search me!)

(10) Go R to wood edge. Join track at cottage then meet track. Go R to A456.

Callow Hill

(11) At church sign, put your back to church & go R 100 yds. After house with double gable ends, take tarmac track L.

(12) Go appx .16 mile to where surface ends, then go ahead on path & take stile.

(13) Take wood path to bottom L corner, then up field edge past

house & take stile L to lane.

(14) Take lane opposite & after 1st house L, take stile R.

(15) Follow R hedge via stiles (1),(2) & (3). Bear R & take stile

● Gorst Hill
>> OPTIONS <<
Routes 18(1) & 20(1)

19

* Gorst Hill to Goodmoorhill

(a) At top field corner, face house, then take stile in R hedge. Cross field & take stile in upper hedge. Go with hedge on your L via stiles to lane.

(b) Go L to junction. Follow drive opposite to take stile. Go R down field edge into wood.

(c) Follow path to upper R corner. Take stile & follow path, becomes lane, to A456.

(d) Go R to track L by church sign.

Callow Hill

(e) At church sign take track past chapel & a few paces on take track L. Pass cottage R & enter wood

(g) Follow main track. CARE; - a few paces in cross faint track - pass 2 tracks L to fork by tree marked "56".

(h) Go L, path slopes down to cross stream.

(i) Go R, pass 3 tracks L to track junction. Go R & take 1st stile L.

(j) Follow woodland path, cross a track, & curve R to meet hedge & take stile L.

(k) Follow wood edge, cross stile & bridge. Go up with fence on your R, take stile (1) R & on via stile (2) to track.

(l) Go R & take gate to field. Bear L to follow wood edge round to take stiles (1) & (2).

(m) Go ahead & take stile to lane. Go L to lane.

(n) Go R, pass carvan site entry & take stile L on R bend.

(o) Go down, cross bridge & follow wood path down L. At bottom DON'T TAKE bridge ahead, go R to bridge.

● Goodmoorhill
>> OPTIONS <<
Routes 7(1), 13(1) & 14(1)

Gorst Hill - Furnace Mill
4.4 miles   7.25 kms

A walk with most of the gorgeous features of Worcestershire landscape, a brook in a deep brown dingle, steep green hills, miles of rolling tree tops seen from a high ridge route, and in the north, the oakwood known as Bell's Coppice.

Furnace Mill sits on the Shropshire/Worcestershire boundary marked by the Dowles Brook. Nearby you cross the trackbed of the railway from Bewdley to Leominster which was abandoned in 1963.

Gorst Hill to Furnace Mill

(1) At top corner of field NB gate with fence on its R. Cross FENCE & then grass to take gate.

(2) Follow track to lane bend & take track L. Pass farm L, go down with wood on your R to its end.

(3) Go R, take gate. Go R round field edge with stream on your R appx .5 mile to track.

(4) Go R to A456. Go L, pass water tower & take next lane R to green gate. DON'T TAKE IT.

(5) Take track R appx .3 mile. Pass bungalow R, curve L to house drive & take gate L into steep field.

(6) Go R & follow upper field edge to take far corner stile R. Go L, pass barn on your R to join track. Follow appx 100 yds to R bend with 2 gates L.

(7) Take R of 2 gates. Go down with hedge on your L & take gate. Pass ruin, go with hedge on your R, curving down L to bottom & find fenced off gap R into dingle.

(8) Cross fence into dingle & follow path with brook on your L to meet it as it bends R.

(9) Cross at shallow point (I hope). Go ahead appx 15 yds with brook on your R to cross low bank with line of trees, into field corner.

(10) Go with line of trees on your L appx 25 yds. (Cross fence (if present, might be temporary). Go up with hedge on your L & take top corner small gate to track.

(11) Go R appx 350 yds to lane bend.

(12) Go ahead, pass lane L to sharp R bend & take gate/stile ahead into forest.

(13) Go ahead, ignore track L, to fence opposite. Take small path L beside it to cross iron stile.

(14) Go up with fence on your L, cross barrier, up to crest & take stile to rough field.

(15) Cross midfield to opposite hedge & take L of 2 gates.

(16) Go down with hedge on your R to gate & A4117 with pub R.

(17) Go L appx 25 yds & take track R. Pass barn R & follow appx .6 mile;
  - past field track R to fork
  - go R to fork (2)
  - go L on path to barrier
  - ignore bridleway sign, keep same line
  - cross railway & up to take gate/stile.

(18) Go with fence/hedge on your R down to take gate to track. Go L to road.

ROUTE 6 RUNS L

(19) Go R to bridge.

●

Furnace Mill
>> OPTIONS <<
Routes 6(a) & 7(a)

20

✳

Furnace Mill
to Gorst Hill

(a) At bridge over Dowles Brook, brook flows S-N just here. Take road W, pass road R to 1st track L

ROUTE 6 RUNS ON AHEAD

(b) Take track L up to farm entrance. Go R & take L of 2 gates.

(c) Go with hedge on your L & take gate/stile into forest.

(d) Cross railway, go up appx 100 yds to where track levels & take path L.

(e) Follow on same line appx .7 mile;
- pass barrier
- pass tracks joining from L, then R
- pass barn L to A4117.

(f) Go L appx 25 yds & take 1st gate R (probably bust).

(g) Go up with hedge on your L & take corner gate. Cross midfield & take stile.

(h) Go down with fence on your R, via barrier, & take iron stile R.

(i) Go with fence on your L. Cross end of track R & take gate/stile to lane bend.

(j) Go ahead, pass lane R to L bend & take green track appx 350 yds to gate across track. DON'T TAKE IT.

(k) Take small gate L & go down with hedge on your R. Cross fence (if present, might be temporary) and on with line of trees L to meet brook.

(l) Go R over low bank, brook on your L, appx 15 yds to shallow point with shelving bank & path opposite.

(m) Cross brook (Good Luck) & follow path with brook on your R & cross fence to field.

(n) Go up L with hedge on your L past ruin. Take gate & up with hedge on your R, take gate to track.

(o) Go R, pass barn on your L & cross fence to take stile R.

(p) Go L along top field edge & down to take gate to drive.

(q) Go ahead, drive becomes track, apx .3 mile to lane. Go L to A456

(r) Go L, pass water tower and take next track R.

(s) Go to end of L fence. Go down L with hedge on your L appx .5 mile, pass stile L & curve R to take gate L onto track.

(t) Go up L, pass farm R to lane bend. Take track R to its end & take gate. Go ahead over grass & cross fence to top field corner.

●

Gorst Hill
>> OPTIONS <<
Routes 18(1) & 19(a)

River Severn Routes (A) & (B)

Walk the west bank. It is slightly more attractive and the only crossing at Severn Lodge and Dowles is by swimming.

I expect that you do not need me to tell you how to follow the River Severn, but here are notes on where to leave the river to join the next route. The Severn flows downstream from Severn Lodge to Arley to Dowles.

>> OPTIONS <<

Severn Lodge: stone arched railway bridge about 150yds from river.

Route 1(8) to Highley & Woodhill or 1(p) to Coppicegate.

Arley: tubular steel footbridge.

Routes 9(a) & 10(1)

Dowles: brook meet Severn by piers of spanless bridge

Route 5(4) to Bewdley or 15(b) to Knowles Mill.